Desperate for God

Trusting God Through Trials

(Thirty Life Lessons)

Glenda Durano

Published by BookCrafters, Parker, CO.
www.bookcrafters.net

Contents

Acknowledgments

Thank you to my friends, family, and mentors for their support of this endeavor: my beloved husband Dee, my heaven-sent daughters and their husbands, my sister and her family, my wonderful mom, Mona, Scott, Jackie, Gary, Pamm, Teresa, Krista, Marie, Roxie, Gerry Wakeland for her encouragement, Lee Warren for patiently dealing with a newbie, my Women of the Word Bible Study, and my Sisters of Strength. Sigh. I could go on and on. I'm so blessed. Thank you, Lord!

Introduction

As a child, I loved participating in Show and Tell. Whether a classmate was exhibiting his prized birthday gift or demonstrating how he fed his pet turtle, I was drawn to real-life examples. Perhaps that's why, in my spiritual life, God has taught me most of my life lessons by using an experience. This was certainly the case in 2012 when my daughter suffered from a devastating condition that eventually rendered her blind. Although I had accepted Christ as my Savior and Lord many years earlier, during that particular time, I became desperate for God. I sought Him with everything in me, and He was always there with a Word or a lesson wrapped in His everlasting love.

Because that was such an intense life experience for me, many of the devotions in this book reflect that period in my life. The overwhelming theme of the lessons I learned during that season was faith; therefore, faith is the focus of many of these devotions. After decades of *believing in* God, I finally learned to *believe* Him. That newfound trust eventually gave birth to spiritual freedom which evolved into a deeper, more abiding relationship with Christ.

After my life had calmed down a bit, I found that I actually missed the intensity of those moments with

God. I also discovered that desperation—having Christ as my only hope—was key to being able to discover God in new ways.

I tend to be easily distracted, so sometimes—okay, lots of times—when I read God's Word, I don't fully understand it the first time around. But God is patient, and He wants me to understand the Bible with both my head and my heart. Therefore, God teaches me the application of His Scripture through life lessons. God's Word is alive and active (Hebrews 4:12). As God reveals Himself to me, I discover the truth of the Scripture. It's as if I suddenly understand not only that 2+2 equals 4, but why it does as well. God *tells* me His truth through His Word; He *shows* me its reality through experience.

That's why this devotional book is written more as a series of stories rather than an exposition of Scripture. As you read these stories, I pray that you will see the truth of God's Word as it is demonstrated through life—especially when we walk through trials.

God longs to show us both Himself and His Truth. In order to do that, Ephesians 1:18 instructs us to open the eyes of our heart. Unfortunately, many times we don't open our spiritual eyes until we're desperate for God—when something in our lives causes us to look for Him again. Praise God; He's always there. Jeremiah 29:13 promises, "You will seek me and find me when you seek me with all your heart." May each of us be desperate for Him every day.

2

Psalm 142:6,7 (MSG)

I CRY OUT, God, CALL OUT:
You're my last chance, my
ONLY hope for life! Oh Listen,
please Listen; I've never been this
low.

Desperate for God

Listen to my cry, for I am in desperate need.
(Psalm 142:6)

Here my Cry, for I am very low.(TLB)

In 2008, my husband owned a successful home building business. We had two loving and obedient daughters; one was attending a private university and the younger was getting ready to graduate a high school nursing program as valedictorian. We had money in the bank and were active in our church. We had health, happiness, and good friends, making us the epitome of the successful family. And we loved God. A lot.

I had always hated keeping a family budget. It was true in 2008, and it's still true today. I don't have the "math gene." But because my husband (who has his MBA) thought it would be a "good idea for me to learn how to keep the family budget," I had that illustrious job. I would procrastinate the task of budgeting for weeks, and when I did get around to it, I frequently made mistakes. It frustrated my husband to no end. One day, he'd had enough.

"Never mind," he announced. "We don't need a budget. We're doing fine."

I was thrilled. Little did we know that less than a

3

year later, my husband would be out of a job and that he wouldn't work for three years.

Although we didn't realize it, we were treating God the same way we were treating our money—we were taking both for granted. Our relationship with God was "fine," just like our budget. Yes, we loved God. He was an important part of our lives. We were blessed and we gave Him credit for our blessings. We sensed His presence often, and we were genuine Christians. Although we loved God, we weren't desperate for Him.

In our minds, we had rationalized that because everything was "fine," we didn't need to be "desperate for God." It seemed as if most of the desperate prayers in the Bible such as Psalm 63:1: "You, God, are my God, earnestly I seek you; I thirst for you. My whole being longs for you in a dry and parched land where there is no water"—had been written in times of turmoil, and that wasn't us. Eventually, we realized that desperate prayer is not a sign of weakness; desperate prayer is a sign of spiritual maturity and was demonstrated by Jacob, Moses, Paul, and even Jesus Christ.

In *Walking with God through Pain and Suffering*, Tim Keller wrote, "You never know Jesus is all you need until Jesus is all you have." Between the years of 2008 and 2014, my husband didn't work for three years; we lost thousands of dollars in the stock market; we were sued in a clawback lawsuit, and one of our daughters suffered a devastating medical condition that eventually caused her to lose her vision.

I'm not saying God brought that suffering upon us—I don't believe He did—but God loved us too much to allow us to stay where we were: stuck in self-sufficiency.

In his book *Apologia pro Vita Sua* (1864), John Henry Newman wrote, "Growth is the only evidence of life." Since we were spiritually complacent at that time, we weren't growing. I don't believe we were spiritually dead, either. I was working at a church, for heaven's sake—but we were probably in a spiritual coma: our spirits were functioning, but they weren't developing. God needed to revive us by giving us spiritual CPR and performing supernatural heart surgery.

Medical professionals say that sometimes when they give CPR, they press so hard that they accidentally break a person's ribs in order to save a life. As God pressed on my heart to bring me back to life, it seemed as if He pressed so hard so hard that He broke my heart. He allowed overwhelming circumstances to flood into my life, and I felt as if I were drowning. I could barely breathe. And yet, God was never so close. Psalm 34:18 promises, "The LORD is close to the brokenhearted and saves those who are crushed in spirit."

God Himself was not crushing my spirit, but He was allowing me to be broken by my circumstances. In the process of these severe situations, after many mistakes and much mercy, God gave me new life—or perhaps more accurately, we received the revitalization that Christ had waiting for us all the while. Ezekiel 36:26 proclaims, "I will give you a new heart and put a new spirit in you; I will remove from you your heart of stone and give you a heart of flesh. And I will put my Spirit in you and move you to follow my decrees and be careful to keep my laws." God's Word

When God is performing heart surgery, He'd prefer that we cooperate as early as possible so that the operation is less painful. Sometimes, however, it takes a while to learn teamwork, but eventually, we do. God makes sure of that. If you are a child of God, He will do whatever it takes to bring you closer to Him. Our lives would be easier, however, if we became desperate for God.

Will It Be Okay?

"Are not two sparrows sold for a penny?" He asks. "Yet not one of them will fall to the ground outside your Father's care. And even the very hairs of your head are all numbered. So don't be afraid; you are worth more than many sparrows"
(Matthew 10:29-31)

On October 11, 2012, my twenty-one-year-old daughter was admitted to the Burn ICU at Parkland Hospital in Dallas for toxic epidermal necrolysis syndrome. TENS, as it is better known, is a severe drug reaction that causes the body to attack itself. This rare autoimmune condition causes a person's skin and internal mucus membranes to blister and slough off, leaving the body defenseless, eventually killing 40% of its victims.

My daughter Amberle had done nothing wrong. She had taken one dose of a common, over-the-counter pain medication—and her body reacted violently—for no known reason and with no known cure.

For weeks, I sat next to my daughter's hospital bed, wondering if she would survive.

Throughout her weeks in the hospital, we wondered

if life would ever be the same. We discovered later that it never would be. As a result of TENS, Amberle experienced numerous chronic health issues, and, most devastating of all, blindness.

Eventually, Amberle learned to adapt. Losing sight is physically and emotionally devastating for anyone, but for Amberle, it was spiritually overwhelming as well. Amberle had been called to medical missions at the age of seven, and her life had been dedicated to that purpose. When Amberle became ill, she had been completing her BSN/RN and now, she felt confused and abandoned by God—cheated by the enemy.

While overcoming her medical issues was a struggle, Amberle's biggest battle was with God—or more accurately, her battle was with God's apparent decision to remove her ability to fulfill her dream of serving Him. She wrestled with God for months. Fortunately, wrestling is a contact sport. It brings you face to face with your opponent. I believe God would rather have us wrestle with Him than just give up and walk away. He wants us to come close. He wants us to know that although "it" may not be okay, we will be because God cares about us more than He cares about our circumstances.

In today's verses, Jesus addresses life's challenges. He assures His disciples of God's constant and deep care.

Throughout Amberle's illness and recovery, we knew God loved her. However, when you're going through a difficult time, especially one that seems contrary to God's purposes, you question His sovereignty. As

Christians, we knew God would never allow anything to happen that could not be used for His glory and our benefit (Romans 8:28-29), but at the time, we didn't see how a devastating illness and long-term suffering could possibly work into His plan. We just wanted God to make "it" all okay.

In his sermon, "The Life Worth Living for Christ is a Life Worth Losing," Pastor Matt Chandler, President of the Acts 29 Network, said, "Comfort is the god of this generation. Therefore suffering is seen as a problem to be solved rather than a providence from God."

God is fully aware of every struggle we encounter—natural ones and supernatural ones. Personally, I don't believe God caused Amberle to become ill. I believe it was an attack from the enemy. God allowed the attack, however, because He knew He could turn it around for His greater glory and our greater good.

As of the writing of this devotional, five years after her illness, God has allowed Amberle to remain blind—and today, she is a blind missionary nurse. If Amberle had maintained all of her physical abilities, people would have thought, *She's such a talented young lady, and she has such a heart for God!* As a person without sight, however, there's absolutely no doubt that God is the one who is empowering Amberle to bring hope and healing to the world.

Whatever you're going through right now, remember, you're going *through* it. "It" may not be okay—but *you* will be. And that's what God cares about: you.

Insurance or Assurance?

"For I am convinced that neither death nor life, neither angels nor demons, neither the present nor the future, nor any powers, neither height nor depth, nor anything else in all creation, will be able to separate us from the love of God that is in Christ Jesus our Lord."
(Romans 8:38-39)

My "insurance policy" obviously was not working. I had a regular prayer time with the Lord, attended not one but two weekly Bible studies, served in children's ministries, read the Bible every day (well . . . almost), and yet, here I was, in one of the worst crises of my life. I needed to talk to the guy who "sold me" this policy right away, so I got down on my knees.

Okay, okay, I know Jesus isn't an insurance salesman, but sometimes Christians act like He is, don't we? I mean, honestly, sometimes I think some people pray the prayer of salvation just to get a little "fire insurance"—if you get my drift. Sure, we profess to be okay that "he sends rain on the righteous and the unrighteous" (Matthew 5:45), but when a disaster actually happens to a godly individual, we have a hard time believing it. Looking heavenward, we sigh, "Life just isn't fair!"

The next time a victim mindset bubbles up in your brain, remind yourself to thank God that life *isn't* fair. Yes, that's right. Thank God that life isn't fair. You see, if life were fair, we would all end up in hell. Every one of us. Because that's what we deserve. *That's* what's fair.

Instead of being fair, however, 2,000 years ago, Jesus Christ came to earth and died on a cross to pay the price for our sins. He did this so our sins could be forgiven and we could live eternally with God in heaven. Not hell.

Instead of having a fair God, we have a good God. A God who won't allow anything to happen that He can't turn around for our benefit and His glory. A God who loves us more than we can fathom and who is with us in every single circumstance—especially those that we can't understand and don't seem to be "covered by the insurance plan" that we have consciously or subconsciously developed.

God isn't about plans. He's about relationship. If "doing the right thing" and "having a plan" worked with God, then our relationship with Him would be conditional. But God's love is unconditional. You and I cannot do one single thing in this world to make God love us more or love us less because God's love is dependent on who *He* is. God is Love (1 John 4:8). That's why His love never fails—because it's dependent on our faithful, perfect, unfailing Father. Not on us.

Don't confuse circumstances with the Savior or imaginary insurance with God's assurance. Today's verses are a promise to the believer that nothing can separate us from God's love.

The only plan worth following is the plan that God designed before the foundation of the world—having a deep, abiding relationship and having an eternal home with Him through Jesus Christ our Lord. Yes, God gives us a plan, but don't stop there. Don't simply seek the solution to your situation; seek the Savior.

Whether your circumstance is triumphant or tragic right now, your response should always be the same: trust God. His "assurance plan" is the only one you need.

What is Good?

And we know that in all things God works for the good of those who love him, who have been called according to his purpose. For those God foreknew he also predestined to be conformed to the image of his Son, that he might be the firstborn among many brothers and sisters.
(Romans 8:28-29)

The *Oxford Dictionary* claims that the English language has 171,476 different words. This does not include 47,156 "obsolete" words—but, hey, who's counting? Oh, that's right. I am.

Of all those words, "set" has the most definitions—with a whopping 464 different meanings. "Run" places a distant second with 396 designations and then comes "go" with 368. No wonder we have so much miscommunication!

Many words have multiple meanings. Most of those definitions are found in dictionaries, but some aren't. Some definitions are very unique—so much so that the precise connotation of a word may only be found in one place: your head. For example, the word "good."

The dictionary defines "good" as "to be desired or approved of." Yet, because we all desire different things at different times, our definition of "good" may be quite distinctive. Additionally, our own meaning of "good" may change depending on the situation. Is a snowstorm good? (If you're at a ski resort, yes; if you have to drive to work, no.) A new job? (Is it a promotion or a demotion?) A new car? (Did you have a wreck?) A funeral? (Was the person a believer?) Depending on the precise situation, any of those circumstances could be viewed as good or bad.

And that's the problem.

Romans 8:28 states, "And we know that in all things God works for the good of those who love him, who have been called according to his purpose." In all things? For the good? Really? Sometimes it just doesn't seem that way, does it? Like…

When the doctor says you have cancer.

When your spouse asks for a divorce.

When you file for bankruptcy.

When your home is destroyed by a natural disaster.

When a fellow Christian is raped or robbed or killed.

How can that be?

Honestly, I don't know. But that's where another important word comes into play: truth.

Truth is what God says about the matter. It's His Word and His Way. Unchangeable and undeniable. Truth is truth, regardless of what you think or feel, and regardless of the circumstance. And because Romans 8:28 is found in God's Word, it's the truth—even if we don't understand it—because God's Word is truth (John 17:17).

During difficult situations, a lot of Christians are confused by Romans 8:28. It's hard to understand how an absolutely tragic situation can eventually work "for the good of those who love him." However, one of the main keys to understanding God's truth is *more* of His truth.

Romans 8:28 is easy to misunderstand unless you read the verse in context, using verse 29 to clarify the meaning of verse 28. Immediately after Romans 8:28, Paul writes: "For those God foreknew he also predestined to be conformed to the image of his Son, that he might be the firstborn among many brothers and sisters." In other words, all things really do work together for good as we become more and more like Him.

So, can God use suffering to conform us to His image? Absolutely. Can he use pain? Certainly. Does that mean God *brings* tragedy to our lives? Not necessarily. But if God does allow pain and suffering in your life, you can trust that He will certainly cause it to work "for the good of those who love him" (Romans 8:28).

James 1:2-4 encourages believers: "Consider it pure joy, my brothers and sisters, when you face trials of many kinds, because you know that the testing of your faith produces perseverance. Let perseverance finish its work so that you may be mature and complete, not lacking anything."

I pray that when I meet my Sovereign Lord and King

face to face, I will not lack anything, but the only way that's going to happen is if I am indeed "conformed to the image of his Son." That probably means that at some point in my life I will "face trials of many kinds." But praise God, He is faithful to stand with me during my trials in order to help me become perfect and complete. And that, my friend, is definitely "good."

Recycle, Reuse, Redeem

What is more, I consider everything a loss because of the surpassing worth of knowing Christ Jesus my Lord, for whose sake I have lost all things. I consider them garbage, that I may gain Christ . . .
(Philippians 3:8)

As a green builder, my husband is a firm believer in recycling. He'll use old plastic ice cream containers to hold nails, week-old newspapers to clean windows, and toilet paper rolls to keep electric cords untangled. If he can't find a use for something, he'll obediently separate it into paper, plastic, metal, and glass, and heaven forbid if he finds an empty green bean can in the bin next to the rinsed-out plastic milk cartons. (Yep, it's my bad!)

God is a recycler, too. He wastes nothing.

Since God is the one who orders our steps (Proverbs 16:9), He is also the one who knows exactly what we will need to get through. He knows the end from the beginning (Isaiah 46:10). One of God's primary goals is to equip us so that we can be ready for the next adventure. Or disaster. Or ego-pumping success.

Sometimes when we see something on the horizon, we think, "God, I'm not ready for this." But you are . . . because God would never call you to do something that you aren't equipped for. Sometimes we may hear God calling our name to step into the unknown and we may think like Moses, "Who me? I can't do this." But we can.

This is not to say that we are equipped to do it on our own. Not at all. Equipment comes in many shapes and sizes. Being equipped doesn't mean you are self-sufficient; it means you have the tools that you need when life throws you a curveball. Perhaps you have the office skills to get a new job or you have the compassion to care for a parent who has Alzheimer's or you have the faith to know that God still loves you when your spouse says he or she no longer does. You may be equipped with a particular talent or knowledge—or you may be equipped with the faith to fully depend on God.

That being said, being equipped is different from being ready. We certainly weren't ready for my husband to be out of work for nearly three years, but we were equipped. We knew what God's Word said about the tithe, and we knew that God is our provider, and we knew that we had nothing to fear. A few months later, when we faced an even more difficult situation, we used what we had learned during my husband's season of unemployment to meet our next challenge.

God is efficient. He never wastes a moment. He is faithful to recycle, reuse, and redeem every difficult experience. When we are in the midst of a trial, it's tempting to ask God, "How can I get out of this mess?" A much better question would be, "What can I get out of this mess?"

In every test and every trial (whether He brings it or He simply allows it), God equips you for something later down the line. He could give you a tool for ministry, teach you to resist temptation, or provide you with perseverance. You may not know what He's doing at the time, but ultimately, if you allow it, He will recycle, reuse, and redeem your situation. He will turn your mess into your message and your test into your testimony.

Can You Hear Me Now?

In his defense Jesus said to them, "My Father
is always at his work to this very day,
and I too am working."
(John 5:17)

It used to drive me crazy! From the other end of our house, my husband would yell, "Hey, honey, can you come here a minute? I want to show you something." Usually, it was an email or an article on the computer that he felt would be of interest to me, and since he had a desktop computer, I had to go to him. Sometimes, however, he didn't have anything to show me; he just wanted to ask me a question.

Your spouse's timing can be rotten sometimes, right? You're in the middle of cooking dinner or working on a project—and of course, that's when he calls you. "Sweetie, can you come here, please?"

Sometimes, I'd be in the middle of something and want to avoid the short trek to my husband's home office, or sometimes I was just lazy. I'd yell back, "What do you want?"

Silence.

I'd try again. "Honey, what do you want?"

More silence.

In frustration, I'd stop what I was doing and go to him.

One day, as I was complaining to God about how this seemingly unfair situation had recently escalated, God stopped me. I sensed the Lord saying, "You know why he doesn't answer you when you're halfway across the house, right? It's because he knows you won't be able to fully understand what he is saying until you are face to face."

God was right (duh!). Earlier in our marriage, when my husband had attempted to answer my questions from halfway across the house, he always had to repeat his answer when I was closer because I hadn't heard him properly.

Of course, God knew about that because that's the way I was with God, too. Many times, I would pray quickly to God without really getting into His presence—sort of a "check-the-box" kind of thing. Especially if it was in the morning and I was busy. Or at night and I was tired. Or anytime I had a distraction or could find an excuse.

Oh sure, God heard me because I'm His child, but I was choosing to miss the joy of His presence.

Most Christians have experienced a season when they felt as if their prayers were not being heard—as if every word hit the ceiling and bounced right back: "God, can you even hear me? I don't feel as if you're even listening. Why haven't you answered my prayer? Where are you?"

Silence.

Maybe you need to get closer.

But not so He can hear you. Rather, so you can experience Him.

Effective prayers are not based on whether or not we "feel" like God is listening. And really, they aren't even based on our proximity to God because He's the One who is omnipresent and omniscient.

Two thousand years ago, God left His heavenly throne and made a way for each of us to have a deep, abiding, daily relationship with Him. That's awesome, and yet, sadly, most Christians are more concerned with what God can do for them than how they can get to know Him.

God is sovereign. He loves us. As such, He is continuously functioning on our behalf—regardless of whether we see it or not, just as Jesus promises in today's verse.

Divine silence does not mean divine inactivity. During those times when we are waiting on God (which is most of the time), He invites us to press in. James 4:8 assures us, "Come near to God and he will come near to you," and Psalm 145:18 promises, "The LORD is near to all who call upon him, to all who call upon him in truth."

Don't simply pursue answers. Pursue the Father. He's pursuing you. Run into His open arms and let Him hold you closely in the silence. When you can't see His hand, you can trust His heart.

Handle It

*Indeed, we felt we had received the sentence
of death. But this happened that we might not rely
on ourselves but on God, who raises the dead.*
(2 Corinthians 1:9)

Have you ever felt completely out of control—as
if you were being sucked down a vortex into
God-knows-what kind of horrible circumstance? You
didn't know what to do. You didn't know how to
pray. And you screamed toward heaven, "God, what
is happening?"

When my daughter became gravely ill, friends
tried to reassure me of God's presence and power—
although I didn't sense it at all. They did their best
to inspire me with platitudes like, "God won't give
you more than you can handle," and "Just be strong.
You'll get through."

But the more I tried to be strong, the more out of
control I became. I couldn't handle it. All the strength
that I could muster was not going to change the
situation.

And then I surrendered. Not to the situation, but to
God.

Sometimes God allows a situation that he doesn't intend for us to "handle" so that we can learn to wholly depend on Him. The apostle Paul confirmed this when he penned today's verse. When I say God "allows" a situation, I choose my words very carefully. The circumstance may be a test designed by God—intended to teach us something about God or to equip us for a coming situation. Or it may be an attack from the enemy. Either way, our response should always be one of obedience and trust.

2 Corinthians 12:9-11 promises, "But he said to me, 'My grace is sufficient for you, for my power is made perfect in weakness.' Therefore I will boast all the more gladly about my weaknesses, so that Christ's power may rest on me."

When you are in the midst of a downward spiral, do you believe that God's grace is sufficient for you? Do you allow His power to rest on you or do you refuse His grace by focusing energy on your own efforts? God's grace is not simply, as the old adage says, "God's riches at Christ's expense." God's grace is power—the power to surrender to His sovereignty. The power to trust. The power to fully depend on Him.

What does that look like in practical terms? Well, it doesn't mean that you become a limp noodle. In fact, surrendering to God requires an enormous amount of courage and strength because you will be going against the flow of every natural inclination known to man. It means that you focus on His ability and His strength—and regardless of how the circumstance appears, you trust Him completely. We can transform life's most challenging obstacles into opportunities that will ultimately bring us closer to God. But we must stay the course and rely on His grace rather than our strength. Let God handle it.

Control Freak

"For my thoughts are not your thoughts,
neither are your ways my ways," declares the LORD.
"As the heavens are higher than the earth,
so are my ways higher than your ways and my
thoughts than your thoughts.
(Isaiah 55:8-9)

I am a control freak—especially when my husband is driving! I admit it, and if we were all honest, I think we would come to the conclusion that we are all control freaks! Even low-energy, laid-back people want a little influence: choices, options. After all, God gave us our brains. He intends us to use them, right?

Well, yes. And no.

We acquired our ability to make choices as a gift from God. Free will. Likewise, we inherited our innate desire to control, but from a much different source: Adam and Eve. Sinful nature.

In the garden of Eden, God gave man a choice: "You are free to eat from any tree in the garden; but you must not eat from the tree of the knowledge of good and evil, for when you eat from it you will certainly die" (Genesis 2:16-17).

And yet, as we all know, when Eve was tempted (Genesis 3:4-5), she and Adam ultimately decided that they wanted to determine what was good and what was evil. Adam and Eve didn't want God to be "in control." They wanted to decide for themselves. Big mistake! (And we've been paying for it ever since!)

Our inherited inclination to control our circumstances becomes most evident when we are overwhelmed by life. We think we've done nothing "wrong," but we're headed towards a catastrophe. We try to figure out "why" something is happening. Is it good or is it evil? Heaven knows it certainly feels evil, but could this be a test from the Lord? An act of discipline? Or is it a ruthless attack from the enemy? And if so, where's God in all this?

We cry out, "God, where are you? Why is this happening? How can I get out of this mess?" Often, the only answer we receive is silence.

Could it be that we are asking the wrong questions? Like Adam and Eve, we want to judge the situation by our own standards instead of trusting God with His. But that's not our job. It's not our job to try to figure out what God is doing. Our job is trust our wise, loving, faithful heavenly Father—knowing that He will not allow anything to occur that He can't turn around, with our cooperation, of course, for our benefit and His glory. And believe me, when you're in the midst of a tragic circumstance, fully trusting God will require every ounce of energy that you have; you simply won't have the strength to try to figure out God.

Not only is fathoming God "not our job," it's also futile. Thankfully, we have no chance of success in that endeavor. You see, if God were small enough for us to comprehend, He would be too small for our problems. If I could fully understand God and His ways, I would no longer need Him. And that's just not going to happen because, indeed, as today's verses remind us, His ways are higher than mine.

When you stop trying to figure out God and start trusting Him more, you'll find that your question marks straighten out into exclamation points. You'll know who's in control—and you'll be glad it's not you.

Freedom through Fire

*"When you pass through the waters,
I will be with you; and when you pass through
the rivers, they will not sweep over you. When you
walk through the fire, you will not be burned;
the flames will not set you ablaze."*
(Isaiah 43:2)

Winston Churchill is credited with saying, "When you're going through hell, keep going."

Although sometimes we may feel otherwise, nothing we experience in this lifetime even comes close to the torment of hell. Scripture does, however, confirm that sometimes we will feel as if we are going through fire, but when we do, we will not be destroyed, just as today's verse promises.

In scientific terms, fire never actually annihilates things. It just stirs up the molecules until they are released from one another. Fire is a chemical reaction between oxygen and some type of fuel (such as wood or gasoline) that occurs when the fuel is heated. I'll spare you the details, but basically, fire is simply molecules and atoms breaking up. What we experience—the flames, the smoke, the heat—are the results of the chemical reaction.

Fire can be viewed as destructive or productive, depending on what is separated. We can all think of numerous instances in which fire is destructive, but examples of fire being productive may be a little more difficult to determine—although they're around us all the time, both large and small.

What about when you're on a camping trip and need to sterilize a needle to remove a splinter? Many times, that can be accomplished by waving the needle over the flame of a match to remove the bacteria and germs. Iron ore is not worth much on its own, but when it is smelted, purified, and combined with carbon, it becomes one of the strongest man-made substances on the planet: steel.

Gold is an element—something only God can create. In its natural state, gold has limited value, but once it has been refined by a 1,000-degree-or-more fire, it is considered a precious metal. The higher the heat, the more the impurities (called dross) can rise to the top to be removed. In fact, that's the difference between 10-, 14-, and 24-karat gold. Twenty-four karat gold (the most valuable) has been purified using the highest flame. In order to be considered a treasure, gold must be separated from the "less precious" dross by fire.

Since this is a devotional and not a science book, hopefully, you know where I'm going with this. People can be refined by fire, too—and although our fires are more figurative than literal, they too can be destructive or productive, depending on whether or not we trust God with the situation. Sometimes God has to take us through the fire in order to purify us—to separate us from some things that He knows will ultimately destroy us. Or He may take us through the fire to strengthen us—like steel.

Other times, God doesn't bring the fire (the enemy does or our bad choices do), but He will allow us to go through it because He knows He can work all things together "for the good of those who love him, who have been called according to his purpose." (Romans 8:28).

Remember Shadrach, Meshach, and Abednego—Daniel's three friends who were thrown into the fiery furnace (literally) because they would not worship the statue of King Nebuchadnezzar (Daniel 3)? They were tied up by "some of the strongest soldiers in his army" and thrown inside a furnace that had been heated "seven times hotter than usual" (Daniel 3:19-20).

Shadrach, Meshach, and Abednego did not get burned in the fiery furnace because there was a fourth man in the fire with them, Jesus Christ. The only things that were actually destroyed in the fire were the ropes that secured them—the things that held them in bondage. When Shadrach, Meshach, and Abednego were freed from the furnace, King Nebuchadnezzar and all his royal advisors saw that "the fire had not harmed their bodies, nor was a hair of their heads singed; their robes were not scorched, and there was no smell of fire on them" (Daniel 3:27).

God did not extinguish the fire or immediately deliver them out of the situation. Shadrach, Meshach, and Abednego had to go through the fire, but God used it for a greater purpose. When God allows you to go through a fire, you can trust Him. He will take you through it and will only allow the things that need to be separated from you—fear, worry, doubt, insecurity, sinful behaviors—to be destroyed. When you trust God, He will bring you freedom through the fire.

Credit Where Credit Is Due

My troubles turned out all for the best—
they forced me to learn from your textbook.
(Psalm 119:71-72 The Message)

When disaster strikes or a situation turns sour, do you automatically assume that the source is spiritual? Usually, it is . . . because our physical world is inextricably linked with the supernatural world. All one has to do is be slightly familiar with the Bible in order to realize that. Our supernatural enemy, Satan, was at the core of Adam and Eve's fall, Job's suffering, and Jesus' temptation in the wilderness—and many times, he's at the root of our troubles today. Yes, the enemy can definitely bring disaster upon us, but sometimes, I think we give him more credit than he deserves. Could there be another explanation for our trials?

God has the ability, the power, and the desire to abundantly bless His children. He can make life incredibly easy for us—one without a care in the world. You may be thinking, *Hey, I'd like to try that for a while.* But while an easy life may be pleasurable and relaxing for our souls, it can be devastating to our spirits. If life were always comfortable, what sort of

Christians would we be? Would we collapse at the first sign of a challenge? Would be able to minister to others in need? Would we be too lazy to spend time with God because we mistakenly believe that we don't need Him?

Sometimes God allows us to go through difficult times because He wants us to exercise our muscle of faith. He wants us to become strong in our dependency on Him. Much like physical exercise, experience is always the best teacher when it comes to growing with God. A person can know exactly how to do pushups and crunches in his mind, but until he actually gets out there and does them, the exercise is not going to change him. Tests and trials tend to drive us to our knees, and as we pray, we become closer to God. Prayer may not always change the situation, but it always changes the one who is praying. And many times, it also changes those who are watching.

Sometimes we spend so much time trying to determine the source of our problems—whether it's God or the devil—that we forget about the goal of our difficulties. Every obstacle that we encounter is an opportunity to trust God more. Whether your challenge is a test from God or a temptation from the enemy or a trial brought about by your own human weakness, the important thing is how you respond: ideally, you'll do so in faith, as a child of God surrendered to His sovereignty.

No matter how mature we are as Christians, most of us are still surprised when God stretches us. We normally assume our hardships are from the enemy.

But don't give Satan more credit than He deserves. As long as we're on this earth, God has a plan for us, so He will continue to grow us for His purpose. We may not see the benefit in the midst of our troubles, but the reward is on the other side. We just have to grow through it. Instead of focusing on the source of our difficulties, let's focus on the result. After all, it's not where you start; it's where you finish.

A New Day

*"See, I am doing a new thing! Now it springs up;
do you not perceive it? I am making a way in the
wilderness and streams in the wasteland."*
(Isaiah 43:19)

Sitting under the New Mexico sky, away from the
glow of the city lights, I stare upward, fascinated
by the stars. It's amazing to think that even during the
day, the stars are still shining in heaven; we just can't
see them until it's dark.

Sometimes it's that way with God, too. As long
as life is bright and cheery, we don't really see Him
because we aren't looking for Him. But when physical,
emotional, or spiritual darkness comes, we seek Him
desperately. Fortunately, Jeremiah 29:13 promises,
"You will seek me and find me when you seek me
with all your heart." Many times, the more extreme
our circumstances are, the more clearly we see Him. In
other words, the darker the night, the brighter the light.

Every room in my house has a light. Some fixtures,
like those in my dining room, are grand and glorious,
illuminating the entire room through a shade of
shimmering crystals. Other lights, like the lamp on my

desk, serve a more practical purpose, enabling me to see better so I can do my work more efficiently. The light for which I am most grateful, however, is not the most beautiful or the most efficient. My most beloved light is the tiny blue nightlight that guides me to my bathroom in the middle of the night. When life is the darkest—literally or figuratively—I need light the most.

Even after becoming an adult, I was afraid of the dark. As far as I could tell, there was nothing good about the night: it was cold, hard, and unfriendly. One day, however, as I was reading Genesis 1, I noticed the wording God used to describe the completion of each day of creation: "And there was evening, and there was morning" (Genesis 1:5).

In Jewish culture, the day begins with evening. As dusk transitions into night, the world grows dark, but then, just as night is at its darkest point, morning breaks into a new day. This mindset carries over to Western culture in our usage of the twelve-hour clock, with 12:00 a.m. (midnight) marking the beginning of a new day. Literally, a new beginning commences at the darkest time.

Spiritually, a new day means that God is stretching you—doing something fresh in you, just as today's verse says. When you're in the dark and can't seem to find your way, it's easy to feel as if you're lost in the wilderness. You may not know where you are, but God does. And He's right there, too—encouraging you to draw near to Him, listen more carefully to Him, and not merely seek His ways but to seek Him.

When Jesus was in the wilderness (Matthew 4:1-11), He was tempted by Satan. It was a difficult and dark time. Although Jesus knew everything, He still ended up in a cruel place of temptation. Why? Because, Matthew 4:1 tells us He "was led by the Spirit."

Although God is Light, He can use the darkness for His purposes. Sometimes, we have to be in the dark to see the Light more clearly. If you're at that point right now, take heart. When it seems as if life can't get any darker, a new day is on its way.

Standing in Joy

Do not grieve, for the joy
of the LORD is your strength.
(Nehemiah 8:10b)

When my twenty-one-year-old daughter lost her vision, we begged for God's intervention. We pleaded for a miracle, and we sought healing through whatever means God would use—all to no avail.

As my daughter began her journey into darkness, we found ourselves having to "defend" ourselves against an unforeseen enemy. Fellow Christians. Feeling a lot like Job, my daughter and our family were accused of "not having enough faith to be healed" or "being disciplined by God." Some verbalized it openly, but others simply hinted at our assumed iniquity.

Friends outside the church attacked God Himself and wanted to know how a loving Father could allow one of His children to be destroyed in this manner. It became all about the *why* instead of the *who*. As a family, we found ourselves not only fighting the challenges of blindness; we also felt forced to justify "His ways" and defend the truth that God was still good, our relationship with Him was strong, our faith was in Him (not healing), and as much as we wanted our daughter to regain her sight, we could still love God without loving God's ways.

Ephesians 6:13 admonishes us to "put on the full armor of God, so that when the day of evil comes, you may be able to stand your ground, and after you have done everything, to stand." We felt as if we had done everything according to God's Word; therefore, instead of spending our time defending His ways (which we didn't fully understand anyway), we resolved to simply stand strong.

We refused to let the enemy steal our joy, and consequently, His joy became our strength, as today's verse mentions. It was okay that we didn't know the answer to the *why* questions as long as we knew *who*: Who was sovereign, Who was good, Who was faithful, and Who loved us "with an everlasting love" (Jeremiah 31:3). God.

Refusing to let fear or doubt stop her, my daughter continued to pursue what she considered to be her calling: nursing. Even though she was blind.

She adjusted her course of study from clinical nursing to public health (which did not require visual abilities), and when she graduated eighteen months later with an MSN-MPH from Johns Hopkins University (and a 4.0), everyone was amazed.

Our understanding of God fails miserably when we try to justify the *whys* of life. God is beyond our rationale—and sometimes all we need to do is stand.

When others see us standing firm, especially when we're in the midst of trials, our joy becomes a testimony of God's reality. As we forge ahead in faith, we defeat the enemy, and we stand in the truth, proving that the joy of the Lord really is our strength.

Broken Pieces

*Therefore, if anyone is in Christ, the new creation
has come: The old has gone, the new is here!*
(2 Corinthians 5:17)

I have a daughter who is a bona fide packrat. Christina has a vast array of "collections"—ranging from her assortment of crumpled "special occasion" paper napkins to over eighty stuffed animals. One of her largest and oldest compendia is an assortment of figurines that has roses on them because her middle name is Rose. Even as a young child, Christina loved her "stuff," and one of the reasons we tolerated her addiction to paraphernalia was because she was always quite meticulous in her care of these articles.

One day, when Christina was about nine years old, I heard a blood-curdling scream from the top of the stairs.

"Mom," Christina shrieked, "Amberle broke my cross! The one with the rose on it!"

From the sound of it, you would have thought that Christina's younger sister, Amberle, had slashed the Mona Lisa instead of breaking a six-inch high glass cross that I had purchased at Love's Country Store.

But to my nine-year-old daughter, the damage was devastating.

Although Amberle apologized profusely, Christina's heart was as broken as the cross had shattered.

"Please, Mom, can you fix it?" she begged as she methodically placed every shard of glass on the kitchen counter.

I looked into her eyes that were brimming with tears. Although I knew that restoring broken figurines was not within my realm of mommy superpowers, I agreed to try. That night, after she went to bed, I got out the superglue and went to work. As I attempted to fix Christina's treasure, my mind was not on the shattered cross, but on my broken life. Our family was in the midst of personal and financial trials, and the stress was definitely taking its toll.

The next morning, when I went to check the cross, I found that the adhesive had not held, and the cross was still fragmented. But Christina was adamant.

"You've got to fix it, Mom. Try again. Please."

I wondered how she had gotten so attached to this $11.00 gift. The next night, as I was trying to repair the irreparable, I saw something catch the light on the corner of the kitchen counter. It was a small sliver of glass that I'd missed the night before. Inserting it carefully into the puzzle of pieces, I glued the cross together again, hoped for the best, and went upstairs to bed.

The next morning, I was shocked to find the cross standing strong on the kitchen counter. I examined it, quite amazed, and whispered a prayer, "God, I wish you could fix my life like that." As if He were standing right next to me, I heard God say, "I would . . . if you would give Me all the pieces."

Has your life been shattered by unexpected difficulty? Are you overwhelmed by illness, loss, or failure? Are you trying to fix the situation yourself or have you surrendered it to the Savior? God wants us to give Him everything. He longs for us to demonstrate our trust in His sovereignty and care, but as long as we insist on keeping our heartaches and hurts or to ourselves, He can't fix them. We must give our brokenness to God—then He will gladly restore us.

God doesn't just mend a heart that's been crushed or repair a life that's been destroyed. He makes it brand new. But we must be willing to give God everything. It's the divine exchange—our broken pieces for His blessed peace.

Thank You, Lord

Give thanks in all circumstances; for this
is God's will for you in Christ Jesus.
(1 Thessalonians 5:18)

A number of years ago, my husband entered a business partnership with several friends. He did not sense the Holy Spirit's leading in the venture, but his friends talked him into it. The business ended up being a disaster, and my husband lost a lot of money. I remember the day he told me that he decided to get out of the business. He was distraught and apologetic for losing so much of our savings. I didn't know what to say; he seemed beyond comfort. Then, the Holy Spirit put the words in my mouth that my husband needed to hear.

"Well," I said in a cheery tone, "at least we still get to go to heaven."

My husband smiled, and then he began to laugh. We realized that we still had a reason to be thankful as long as we put everything in perspective.

Satan wants to steal our gratitude. In the garden of Eden, Eve had everything she could possibly want, but she focused on what she couldn't have. Her thanklessness caused her to become disgruntled and dissatisfied—a dangerous mindset. God knows that an absence of appreciation can lead to sin. This is why He doesn't merely suggest that we are thankful: He commands it!

Psalms 106:1, 107:1 and 118:1 all begin with the same admonition: "Give thanks to the LORD, for he is good." I think that if God repeats Himself three times, it's pretty important, don't you? In fact, Scripture reminds us to be thankful multiple times:

Psalm 100:4 says, "Enter his gates with thanksgiving and his courts with praise; give thanks to him and praise his name." (It starts with thanksgiving!)

Colossians 3:17 says, "And whatever you do, whether in word or deed, do it all in the name of the Lord Jesus, giving thanks to God the Father through him." (Be thankful for what you are doing.)

Philippians 4:6 says, "Do not be anxious about anything, but in every situation, by prayer and petition, with thanksgiving, present your requests to God." (Even in times of need, be thankful.)

Being grateful to God seems like it should be easy. He's given us so much, but sometimes, when life's circumstances are hard, being thankful is difficult. People die, children get sick, spouses are unfaithful, people lose money. Simply put, sometimes life sucks. Fortunately, the apostle Paul did not say that you need to be grateful *for* miserable circumstances; he only said that you need to be grateful *in* them: "Give thanks *in* all circumstances; for this is God's will for you in Christ Jesus" (1 Thessalonians 5:18 emphasis added).

It is God's will—His desire for us—that Christians should be thankful in all situations. We know that God only wills things for His children that are ultimately beneficial because He loves us (Psalm 103:1-5). Certainly, being thankful creates a more positive attitude, but being thankful also protects us from Satan's snare.

When we're ungrateful, we tend to do two things.

First, we complain. This does not glorify God. Philippians 2:14-15 instructs, "Do everything without grumbling or arguing, so that you may become blameless and pure, 'children of God without fault in a warped and crooked generation.' Then you will shine among them like stars in the sky."

We also tend to compare our circumstances with others' situations and focus on how God is "just not fair" and we deserve more. This is our pride speaking because, in truth, the only thing we *deserve* is eternal punishment in hell (Romans 3:23, Romans 6:23).

For many people, thankfulness is dependent on the situation, rather than the presence of the Savior. When you are going through a tough time, be grateful that God is with you. He will guide you in every circumstance (Psalm 32:8), and He will never leave you (Hebrews 13:5). You can be thankful for that!

I Have a Problem

Oh, magnify the LORD with me,
and let us exalt his name together!
(Psalm 34:3 ESV)

Cancer. Divorce. Bankruptcy. Loss. Illness. So many problems. So many prayers.

We all need something: healing, wisdom, financial favor, a restored relationship.

So we pray, asking God to answer to meet our needs because we *know* He can (Philippians 4:19).

Time passes. We continue to pray, but the problem still exists . . . and we wonder, *Where is God?*

The answer is simple. God is right there with you—right where He always is. It's just that we can't see Him because we've become so focused on the problem.

First Samuel 17 tells the familiar story of David and Goliath: the account of a young shepherd boy who defeats the Philistine giant and saves the nation of Israel. On the surface, the story appears to be the epic chronicle of an underdog turned hero. Going a little bit deeper, however, we can appreciate the story not just because the "good guy" wins, but because we all know what it's like to have a Goliath in our lives. A problem that seems insurmountable. A difficulty that occupies our thoughts and energies. A situation overflowing with fear and worry. Something so big that it's difficult to see anything else.

That's what happened to the Israelites. Yes, Goliath was a big guy, a formidable opponent. The challenge was real but that was all the Israelite army could see. They didn't realize that Goliath was "blocking their view" of the only One who could save the Israelites: God Himself. All they saw was a huge, impossible situation in the form of a giant.

David, on the other hand, saw a huge God. He realized the earthly obstacle but focused on the divine opportunity. "The battle is the LORD's," David declared to Goliath shortly before casting his lethal stone, "and he will give all of you into our hands" (1 Samuel 17:47).

Years later, David wrote the words we find in today's verse.

When you face a difficulty, what do you magnify? Do you focus on your fear? Emphasize the issue instead of the "I am?" Allow worry to win over God's Word?

Having the right perspective makes a world of difference when circumstances are difficult. Yes, life is hard. The challenge is real. But God is sovereign.

Magnifying the Lord is a choice—a spiritual discipline. It doesn't mean that you put on rose-colored glasses and pretend that the problem doesn't exist. It means that you recognize the issue, but you choose your perspective. The problem may be big, but God is bigger.

Magnifying the Lord means remembering both God's promises and God's personality. God is good (Psalm 118:1), loving (1 John 4:8), faithful (1 Corinthians 1:9), and kind (Romans 11:22). God promises to be with you (Isaiah 41:10), to fight for you (Exodus 14:14), and to make your paths straight (Proverbs 3:6). Magnifying the Lord means taking all those problem-focused thoughts captive (2 Corinthians 10:5) and instead, choosing to "set your mind on things above" (Colossians 3:2). It's not easy. But you can do it.

Throughout Scripture, we read verses like "I *will* praise the Lord" (Psalm 146:2 emphasis added), "I *will* put my trust in you" (Psalm 56:3 NLT emphasis added), and I *will* give thanks to you, LORD" (Psalm 9:1 emphasis added). These words were not written when life was easy; they were penned in crisis. The psalmist made a choice to magnify the Lord in the midst of hardship.

Next time you're faced with a Goliath-sized glitch, change your perspective. Magnify the Lord. Let your vision lead you to victory by focusing on the Word's promises instead of the world's problems.

This Is a Test

Consider it pure joy, my brothers and sisters,
whenever you face trials of many kinds . . .
(James 1:2)

I've never met anyone who enjoys a test—not really. I think the reason most people don't enjoy tests is that they don't like being told they're wrong. Taking a test can be an unpleasant, ego-deflating experience, especially after the test is graded, and we see all those red checkmarks on the page. I mean, we tried our best, didn't we? But unfortunately, we didn't get everything right. Tests *are* necessary, however, because the first step to learning anything is recognizing what you don't know. Sometimes, the only way to discover that is through a test.

In today's verse, James refers to God's tests. His tests always involve making a situational choice. We can react to the circumstance with worry, fear, jealousy, resentment, self-sufficiency, impatience, anger, or frustration, in an attempt to justify our behavior due to the occasion, *or* we can choose God's way. We can choose to worry or to trust; demonstrate patience or impatience; show joy or misery; or employ kindness or cruelty.

When I choose my way instead of God's way, it's usually because I am focusing on the situation rather than the Savior in the storm. Oddly enough, God can use that very same storm to strengthen my relationship with Him if I choose to depend on Him. But it's my choice: I can choose to draw closer and learn about Him, or I can remain in detached ignorance. First Corinthians 10:13 promises that I *can* pass the test without reverting to my sinful choices: "When you are tempted, he will also provide a way out so that you can endure it." The question is, *Will I?*

God develops our Christian character through testing—by giving us an opportunity to express the exact opposite quality. For example, He tests our love by putting us into a relationship with a very unlovable person. He develops our peace by allowing our lives to fall apart. In each of these situations, the only way we can pass the test is to choose the right answer: to trust and depend on God.

First Peter 1:7 says that such trials " have come so that the proven genuineness of your faith—of greater worth than gold, which perishes even though refined by fire—may result in praise, glory and honor when Jesus Christ is revealed." Contemplating the tests that God gives us for the purpose of bringing Him praise may stir up a bit of anxiety in some of us. We know that God knows that we can succeed if we make the right choices, but what if we don't? What if we make the wrong choice and end up failing? Well, simply put, that's not going to happen because, in God's classroom, you never fail. You just get to take the test over and over and over again.

Sometimes, I've found myself asking God, "Why does this always happen to me?" The answer is clear: because God is merciful, and He's giving me another chance to learn that lesson that I haven't yet learned in order to build a stronger relationship between Him and me.

Sometimes, life's tests aren't just difficult; they're heartbreaking. But because God knows the future and sees what we can become if we cooperate with Him in our time of testing, He allows it. Even if God does not bring the test Himself (e.g., it's a consequence of our sinful behavior or the enemy launching a spiritual attack against us), in His sovereignty, God may allow a seemingly impossible test: cancer, infidelity, bankruptcy, loss, death, illness, or disability. The situation will be more than you can handle but remember: God can handle it, and He wants you to depend on Him.

Regardless of the specific "right answers" in your particular test, the correct underlying response is always the same: *Lord, I trust you.*

Dot to Dot

A person's steps are directed by the LORD.
How then can anyone understand their own way?
(Proverbs 20:24)

When I was a kid, I loved doing dot to dot pictures.
I preferred entertaining myself with dot to dots
rather than coloring books because when you used
a coloring book, you always had to stay inside the
lines—or so I was told. How boring!

I always tried to guess what the image was before
I began. And I was almost always wrong. That was a
good thing because the simple act of moving my pencil
from one numbered dot to another—sometimes clear
across the page—was somehow made more enjoyable
when I didn't know what the end result would be until I
finished. Then with one final stroke, voilà! The ultimate
image appeared.

Sometimes, however, about halfway through the
process, I *thought* I knew what the picture was, so I
ignored the numbers and followed my deficient logic.
That's when I ended up with three-armed teddy bears
or hula dancers without heads. At other times, I became
impatient because I just knew that the dot to dot creator

had made a mistake, and therefore, I had no choice but to add my own dots in order for the picture to make sense—which usually resulted in a creation resembling Picasso's early attempts at cubism. And then there were times when, after completing every connection correctly, I still had no clue what the picture was.

That's why, to me, life is like a giant dot to dot. Except, of course, we are not the artists. We are at the heart of the picture. God is the ultimate Creator and, as He provides us with defining moments—choices we make day in and day out—we travel from dot to dot.

Sometimes, He guides us very distinctly, and His direction is clear. At other times, we have choices and may be tempted to add our own dots or go our own way. (Beware the three-armed teddy bears!) Occasionally, it seems as if we are somewhere in between the dots because we are waiting for the next stroke of the pen.

The point is, as human beings, our tendency is to want to design our own dot to dot destiny. And while we must be proactive in order to achieve life's goals, we are not the artists of our own fate. Each of us is a highly valued, extraordinarily unique creation, constantly in the process of becoming a masterpiece as we yield to the Master Creator. What's even more exciting, however, is the fact that we are creations who have the opportunity to become *children* of the Creator as we trust Him with our lives. John 1:12 promises, "Yet to all who did receive him, to those who believed in his name, he gave the right to become children of God."

In geometry, we learn that the shortest distance between two points is a straight line. While that may be true in the dot to dot of life, sometimes, the shortest distance isn't always the best route.

Sometimes, we have a result in our mind—our own picture of what life should look like, usually in the form of a career or dream goal—and we impatiently think that the best way to get from Point A to Point Z is by going straight to it. However, if we try to bypass Points B through Y and take a shortcut, cursing God for the unexpected dots He places in our lives, we may not be ready for point Z when we ultimately get there. God wants to teach us something on Points B, C, and so on, and sometimes those lessons are hard. As His children, however, we can trust that He knows our every need (Matthew 6:8).

God created you in love and custom-designed your path (Jeremiah 29:11). Every dot delivers direction and every point has a purpose. And although you may not be able to see the how a particular experience fits into the overall picture, God does, and He never wastes a moment. Like a skilled craftsman, God is at work, conforming you to the image of His Son (Romans 8:29). Rather than trying to take a detour or objecting to His intentions, we would be wise to agree with Isaiah 64:8: "Yet you, LORD, are our Father. We are the clay, you are the potter; we are all the work of your hand."

No matter where you are in your dot to dot life—at a place of clarity or a crossroad of confusion—your job is to listen to the Creator and walk in the Spirit. We must trust our Heavenly Father as the Master Artist— the only One who knows exactly what dots are needed to complete the perfect picture of our purpose.

Do the Right Thing

*And without faith it is impossible to
please God, because anyone who comes to
him must believe that he exists and that
he rewards those who earnestly seek him.*
(Hebrews 11:6)

Have you ever felt as if you were "doing the right thing" when you were suddenly blindsided by trouble? You were a loving wife and mother but your husband left you. You were a hardworking employee but you were laid off. You were a devoted follower of Christ but an illness destroyed you. You thought you were pressing "on toward the goal to win the prize for which God has called" you (Philippians 3:14) when you suddenly hit a roadblock. Did you question God and wonder how He could allow it?

You're in good company. John the Baptist was doing the right thing when He was thrown in prison. He sent His followers to question Jesus about whether or not He was really the Messiah (Matthew 11:1-11). Moses had stepped out and obeyed God but when the results were different from what he expected, he wanted to quit (Exodus 5:15-23). Shortly after Elijah had been victorious on Mount Carmel, he asked God to take His life (1 Kings 18-19). All were heroes of the faith who asked God, *Why?*

What was wrong with these great men of faith? Nothing, really. They were simply human, and their momentary circumstances led them to temporarily doubt God.

Doubt can be dangerous. When doubt is not resolved, it can lead to sin, as it did in the garden of Eden (Genesis 3:1). Doubt can become unbelief but it is not the same as unbelief. Doubt arises in the context of faith. It is a longing to be sure of the thing in which we trust. Doubt is usually brought on by hard circumstances and is a product of our thoughts. Unbelief, on the other hand, if it is true unbelief, is often rooted in pride and is the result of a willful decision. It's a choice of the heart—a choice to reject God.

God gives us the remedy for doubt: faith. Faith comes from knowing God—most often, through prayer and Scripture meditation. Trust is developed through relationship, and more than anything, that's what God desires, as the author of today's verse describes. The reward that the believer receives is a deeper, more intimate relationship with Christ—a relationship that is built on solid faith and can stand the storms of doubt.

When handled properly, doubt can open a dialogue with God and bring us closer to Him. Consider one of the greatest skeptics in Scripture: the disciple Thomas, who is remembered primarily for his doubt. Christ did not reprimand Thomas for his doubt. He dispelled

Thomas's doubt by inviting him to learn the truth. "Put your finger here; see my hands," the Risen Lord told Thomas. "Reach out your hand and put it into my side. Stop doubting and believe" (John 20: 24-29). In Mark 9:14-29, when the father of a demon-possessed boy experienced doubt, he begged Jesus to help him overcome his unbelief. Jesus obliged by miraculously healing his child.

As believers, we must train ourselves to look at the person and the promises of God rather than the problems of this world. Even if we are doing the right thing, because we live in a fallen world, "wrong things" may occur. Obstacles to our faith ("wrong things") can become opportunities for the Father to demonstrate His grace, mercy, and love as well as opportunities for us to develop our faith.

Faith doesn't necessarily grow when everything is going our way. Faith matures when we *don't* get what we want, and we decide to trust God anyway. Our disappointments become God's appointments and our interruptions; His intervention. Even if the wrong thing happens when you're doing the right thing, God always promises to produce the right result: a deeper relationship with Him through faith.

Why?

*Now faith is confidence in what we hope for
and assurance about what we do not see.*
(Hebrews 11:1)

When something tragic happens, especially to a
believer, we struggle with the *why* question. We
know that God loves us, so this doesn't make sense
because when somebody loves us, it's supposed to feel
good, isn't it?

I suppose if our world were built on feelings, that
would be correct, but the truth is, as Christians, our
world is not built on feelings; it's built on something
much more secure: faith. Today's verse defines faith for
us: it is confidence in what we hope for and assurance
about what we do not see. Faith is more secure than
feelings because feelings change—sometimes in an
instant and sometimes over time.

Feelings are usually dependent on circumstances
and whether we perceive those circumstances as
good or bad. Faith, on the other hand, doesn't rely
on the situation because faith is not built on your
evaluation of a situation; faith is formed through
your relationship with Jesus Christ. The question you

have to ask yourself is, *Can I trust God in this—even if I don't know the outcome?* The answer, of course, is a resounding yes, because although circumstances and feelings change, God does not. Faith is not dependent on answers. Faith is dependent on God.

Hebrews 11 is known as "The Hall of Faith." In it, the writer lists hero after hero whose faith was rewarded—who received strength and power to do extraordinary things with spectacular results, all to the glory of God. I don't know about you, but sometimes I've looked at those first thirty-four verses of Hebrews 11 and asked, "What about me, God? Don't I have enough faith? Can't you do that for me, too? Give me an amazing result that will glorify you!"

But then I read the remaining six verses of the chapter and I see that sometimes the reward of faith is that God blesses those He loves with the grace to endure horrible circumstances, all to His glory.

In my opinion, that's when the true test of faith comes because faith isn't about getting what you want; faith is about trusting God, regardless of the situation. The ultimate reward of faith is not that a circumstance went your way. The ultimate reward of faith is that God will bless you with eternal life.

Hebrews 11:6 confirms, "Without faith it is impossible to please God, because anyone who comes to him must believe that he exists and that he rewards those who earnestly seek him." Faith is the result of believing that Jesus Christ died for our sins and made a way for us to be right with God so we could spend eternity in heaven. When that truth permeates our lives, we think and act differently.

The only way that a believer can reconcile a world in which bad things happen to good people with a God they can trust is by having faith. You have to trust God and the truth of Scripture more than you trust life itself. Life frequently feels cruel and unloving because it is. Evil abounds in this world, but the existence of evil does not nullify God; on the contrary, it should cause us to seek Him more.

God is love (1 John 4:8) but love does not always feel good. The greatest act of love ever demonstrated on this planet was when Jesus Christ died on a cross to bring salvation to you and me. As He stretched out His arms and nails pierced His hands and His feet and the crowd taunted Him mercilessly, He did not feel good. In fact, three of the Gospels record that Jesus pleaded with God to "remove this cup"—just like we frequently do when we are facing incredible trials. Yet, Jesus ultimately chose faith over feeling when He submitted to the Father by praying for God's will, rather than His own (Luke 22:42, Matthew 26:39, Mark 14:36).

After reading that last paragraph, you may not feel very encouraged. But take heart and take another look. Thank God that Jesus "endured the cross, scorning its shame, and sat down at the right hand of the throne of God" (Hebrews 12:2). That is where our faith comes from, and that same passage encourages us as believers to "run with perseverance the race marked out for us, fixing our eyes on Jesus, the pioneer and perfecter of faith" (Hebrews 12:1-2). That's what it's all about.

Why does God allow pain and suffering for those He loves? I don't know. And I don't believe we will ever know this side of heaven. I do know, however, that God equips His children for whatever situation He calls us to. And that means we walk by faith and believe His promises—even when life doesn't feel right.

Fight the Good Fight

*The weapons we fight with are not the weapons
of the world. On the contrary, they have divine
power to demolish strongholds. We demolish
arguments and every pretension that sets itself up
against the knowledge of God, and we take captive
every thought to make it obedient to Christ.*
(2 Corinthians 10:4-5)

In military strategy, half the battle is knowing who
your enemy is. Throughout history, villains of war
have been known to send out "distractors" in hopes
of diverting their opponent's resources to the wrong
target, attacking a "dummy," so to speak, while the real
enemy wreaks havoc.

Satan knows the rules of war, and he uses them to
his advantage. When we're having marital discord,
we assume the enemy is our spouse; when we're
struggling with a nasty co-worker, we believe our
associate is the origin of our agony; when the church
is divided like a banana split, our deacons suddenly
become like demons, causing mayhem in the ministry.
All the while, we're being distracted from the real
enemy.

Ephesians 6:10-18 clearly confirms that our enemy is Satan—the one who comes to "steal and kill and destroy" (John 10:10). As Christians, although we know that eventually we will win the war (the book of Revelation assures it!), it's easy to feel as if we are losing the battle when we are drowning in depression, attacked by anger, or hounded by hopelessness.

Fortunately, God has given us everything we need to effectively battle with the enemy. In Ephesians 6:14-17, Paul lists our defensive equipment—components of our belief system that protect us from the devil's deception: truth, righteousness, faith, salvation, and peace. As long as we hold onto these and set our mind on things above (Colossians 3:2), we cannot be brought down. Additionally, however, Christians are also given an offensive weapon which, unfortunately, is frequently overlooked: the "sword of the Spirit, which is the word of God" (Ephesians 6:17).

Today's verses remind us that our battle against sin or the devil and his cohorts is not fought with the weapons of this world, but rather, with the Word of God.

When Christians are under attack, frequently they go right to their knees, which is exactly where they should go. They pray and ask for God's help, which is exactly what they should do. But many stop there. They apply truth, righteousness, faith, salvation, and peace—and they survive—but the next day, the enemy comes at them with even more force.

The mistake that Christians make is that they forget that Satan is not omniscient. He can't read our minds.

When a Christian prays silently or thinks about Scripture, although he may be building himself up, he's not actively engaging in combat. As far as the enemy is concerned, that believer is weak—unwilling or unable to fight back. He's like a soldier who has a sword but keeps it in its sheathe.

In order for a Christian to actually wield the sword of the Spirit and attack the enemy, he has to say the Word of God aloud (Jeremiah 23:29, Hebrews 4:6, John 6:63). When Satan senses the sword, he flees (James 4:7). It's not as if you're mystically banishing Satan by using some sort of secret superpower; you're simply doing what the Bible tells you to do: vocally releasing the power of God's Word to accomplish God's will (Isaiah 55:11).

God knows that it can be difficult to recall Scripture when you're under attack, so He makes it easy by promising to inhabit the praises of His people (Psalm 22:3).

Second Chronicles 20 recounts the story of King Jehoshaphat and his army battling against Moab. As they march into combat, God instructs the army to sing praises. Sing praises? Really? Yes, and verse 22 relates, "as they began to sing and praise, the LORD set ambushes against the men . . . who were invading Judah."

If God really does inhabit the praises of His people (as Scripture declares), then when we release our praises, we release God's power. Satan is not going to hang around when we start praising God because he can't stand it! As we confidently recall God's scriptural promises aloud, the sword of the Spirit pierces a hole in Satan's plans and sends him running for cover!

Although Satan may sometimes look like your spouse or co-worker (that's his "cover"), Scripture is clear: Satan is your enemy, and he is already defeated (Colossians 2:15). But Satan is betting on the fact that you don't know that! When the enemy attacks, be powerful in the Lord by using what He's already given you—His Word and His praises. You may be in a battle right now, but take heart, the war is over . . . and Christ has won!

A Pearl of Great Price

*Rejoice inasmuch as you participate
in the sufferings of Christ, so that you may be
overjoyed when his glory is revealed.*
(1 Peter 4:13)

When my husband and I were dating, he gave me a beautiful strand of pearls. I wear them often, not only because they are sentimental, but because they are symbolic. They remind me of how our thirty-one-year-old promise to love, honor, and cherish one another has prevailed over the occasional pain we have provoked as a far-from-perfect couple.

A perfect pearl is the result of pain. A small grain of sand is placed inside an oyster. The sand irritates the lining of the small creature, and since there is no way for the oyster to expel it, in order to relieve the pain, the oyster secretes a substance that coats the grain of sand with a lustrous white layer. Again and again, the oyster strives to relieve his suffering by secreting layer after layer of the material, but his attempts to get rid of the irritant are in vain. In the process of dealing with its pain, however, the oyster produces a beautiful pearl from the source of its irritation, the grain of sand. As far as the oyster is concerned, the pearl represents pain. For the human being who purchases the gem, however, the pearl is a precious reminder of how God can bring profit out of pain.

Pain is never pleasant, but it has a purpose: it can make us more like Christ.

Suffering reduces pride and causes us to become dependent on God. Paul understood this. In 2 Corinthians 1:9, he writes, "Indeed we felt we had received the sentence of death. But this happened that we might not rely on ourselves but on God, who raises the dead." When we don't "get our own way," pain may also reveal our tendencies to commit sin through anger, frustration, and selfishness. Lastly, suffering makes us more like Christ because when we experience pain, we become more compassionate to one another. Second Corinthians 1:4 reminds us that God "comforts us in all our troubles, so that we can comfort those in any trouble with the comfort we ourselves receive from God."

We live in a fallen world. Therefore, every person will experience pain and suffering to some degree. Sometimes our grief is due to God's discipline; sometimes it is a consequence of sin; and sometimes, like Job, it is a result of a demonic attack. Regardless of the reason, I believe that we would be much better off if we initially approached our problems with the recognition that misery *can* be meaningful—as long as we are open to God working in our lives.

God never wastes a moment of our pain. In His ever-efficient manner, God supernaturally corrects and edifies us through suffering, but He also redeems our pain so we can become more Christlike. Our anguish is not only worthwhile; it's beneficial. As today's verse reminds us, when we grasp the purpose of pain, it no longer has to be painful. We will be "overjoyed when his glory is revealed" (1 Peter 4:13).

God's glory will be revealed to His children when they enter His kingdom—a kingdom that is referred to as "the pearl of great price" (Matthew 13:45-46). Is it any wonder that Revelation 21:21 reveals that the twelve gates of heaven are each made of an enormous pearl? It is only due to Christ's pain that those gates exist at all.

What If?

*"If we are thrown into the blazing furnace,
the God we serve is able to deliver us from it,
and he will deliver us from Your Majesty's hand.
But even if he does not, we want you to know,
Your Majesty, that we will not serve your gods or
worship the image of gold you have set up."*
(Daniel 3:17-18)

What if?
These are two of the most dangerous words in the English language and two of the most powerful tools in Satan's arsenal. Words that are fed by fear and can steal our faith.

What if . . .

I don't get well?

My spouse asks for a divorce?

I can't pay my bills?

My child dies?

God doesn't answer my prayer?

What if?

What if takes us into a dark world of future fantasy and away from the present state of life—especially when the present state is far from ideal. We are transported from the reality of *what is* to the illusion of *what if* through deception: the falsehood of fear.

For many of us, fear is an idol. It holds enormous sway over our thoughts and our actions. We become obsessed with it and can't stop thinking about it—and that's what makes fear an idol. Much like the idols of the Old Testament, the idol of fear is man-made. And also like the idols of the Old Testament, it's not real!

Please don't misunderstand. The danger of the circumstance may be absolutely real, but the fear is not. You may be facing divorce, bankruptcy, and death— all situations that come with dire consequences. But the fear that you experience with those circumstances is purely a product of your imagination—a future fantasy, driven by *what if.*

Fear is faith in reverse. Fear means that you believe the enemy more than you believe God. So, whom will you believe? Will you bow down to the falsehood of fear or will you walk through your circumstance with faith?

I've mentioned Daniel 3 previously, but it's a great example of choosing faith over fear, so I'll use it again. When King Nebuchadnezzar insisted that Shadrach, Meshach, and Abednego bow down to an idol, the three Hebrew boys refused. The king threatened to throw them to their deaths into the fiery furnace. The danger was real. Yet, instead of bowing down to fear, the three men provided the answer we see in today's verses, in faith.

Shadrach, Meshach, and Abednego did not know what the result of their decision would be. They could have died. What they did know, however, was that they could not bow down to the idol of fear. The three Hebrew men knew that God was able to save them so, risking their earthly lives, they chose to walk in faith.

When you are faced with a choice between what is and what if, will you make the right choice? Will you refuse to bow down to the idol of fear? Will you walk through life's challenges in faith?

Too Big for a Box

How great is God—beyond our understanding!
The number of his years is past finding out.
(Job 36:26)

The first time our family moved, both of my girls were under four years old. Although they were quite capable of entertaining themselves, they were still kids and they needed my frequent care. Planning ahead, I decided to allow two weeks to pack instead of the recommended one because I figured most of my packing would be done during nap time. I purchased some used boxes, brought them home, and began taping them together. Suddenly, my girls' lives turned into a world of fantasy. Boxes became houses, cars, and castle walls. It was box-mania! Because they were fascinated with the cardboard containers, I packed in record time.

Although we may not always acknowledge it, adults love boxes, too. Boxes tell us what to expect. They are usually labeled, sometimes with vital information regarding the product inside or sometimes with assembly or operating instructions. Even if it's not labeled, the box gives us a clue of what's inside and starts to answer the question, *What is it?*—the constant question we ask as we seek to understand the world.

We do the same thing with God. We try to put Him in a box in order to understand Him or we label Him based on what we see. But God is much bigger than a box and indescribable beyond words. Romans 11:33 proclaims, "Oh, the depth of the riches of the wisdom and knowledge of God! How unsearchable his judgments, and his paths beyond tracing out!" In the same way, Isaiah 40:28 tells us, "His understanding no one can fathom."

So, does that mean we shouldn't even try to understand God? Should we just muddle along in ignorance? Not at all. In fact, Proverbs 4:6-7 admonishes us to do the opposite, "Do not forsake wisdom, and she will protect you," and in the next verse, "Though it cost all you have, get understanding."

At first glance, these verses may seem contradictory to the earlier ones regarding our inability to understand God, but they are not. Think about a relationship with a person. When you love someone, you want to understand him—not so you'll be able to label him or put him in a box but so you can know what pleases that person, so you can communicate better, or so you enjoy your time together. It may take a lifetime to understand that person (and you may feel like you never fully achieve it), but you still keep trying. When you finally understand someone, you feel as if you can trust the motivations behind his actions and ideas.

The mistake that Christians sometimes make is that we feel as if we need to understand God in order to trust Him. We want things to "make sense" so we can be on board with God's plan. If we'd look a little deeper into our motivations, we'd probably see that the reason we want to understand what God is doing is that we don't want to exercise our faith. And yet, faith is the cornerstone of our relationship with Christ. According to Hebrews 11:6, "Without faith it is impossible to please God."

Paul prayed for the believers in Ephesus to have understanding—not so they would have head knowledge but so they would have heart knowledge—spiritual revelation. He prayed, "I keep asking that the God of our Lord Jesus Christ, the glorious Father, may give you the Spirit of wisdom and revelation, so that you may know him better" (Ephesians 1:17). The desire to understand God for the purpose of *knowing* Him is entirely different than the desire to understand God for the purpose of *trusting* Him.

Hebrews 11:1-3 defines faith as the "confidence in what we hope for and assurance about what we do not see." It goes on to say, "By faith we understand that . . ." In other words, it's not through our head that we understand God—it's through our heart, our relationship with Him.

I don't know about you, but I'm glad that we serve an infinite, out-of-the box God who has infinite, out-of-the-box ways. Even when you can't see His hand, you can trust His heart.

Keeping the Main Thing
the Main Thing

But seek first his kingdom and his righteousness,
and all these things will be given to you as well.
(Matthew 6:33)

When my daughter, Amberle, became gravely and chronically ill, I prayed multiple times a day, every day, for her healing. I asked God for His mercy and His miracles. I praised Him for every ounce of progress. I thanked God that He was with us in the journey, and I obediently cast my cares on Him. Eventually, I even praised God for my daughter's illness because He was being glorified in it.

Outside my prayer life, much of my husband's and my energy went to the practical aspects of my daughter's illness. We researched new treatments, verified insurance payments, and blogged about her condition. We had a cadre of prayer partners who wanted to keep updated so they would know how to pray.

When doctors concluded that the disability brought on by Amberle's medical condition (blindness) was probably permanent, I sought guidance from spiritual mentors regarding whether or not I should stop praying for her healing. Although I did not see how Amberle's blindness could possibly be in the perfect will of God, I was willing to accept it, and I did not want to pray for something that might be outside God's plan.

Their response was, "God wants us to bring our concerns before Him. If it matters to you, it matters to Him."

They were right.

So, I kept praying. Every prayer I uttered, whether it was at mealtime or bedtime, while I was in public or in private, mentioned my daughter's illness. I didn't just pray out of habit. I prayed because it meant so much to me. I knew God was fully capable of healing her, and I knew, if God deemed it best, He would heal her. I wasn't upset with God or trying to get my way; I was simply being persistent in prayer. Or so I thought.

In reality, Amberle's healing had become an idol.

It's hard to understand how something "good" can become an idol—something that would seem to glorify God, like a miraculous healing. But an idol is anything that has your heart. Any time a person, event, or thing—no matter how "God-glorifying" it seems to be—occupies more of your heart than God does (as demonstrated through the time, thoughts, energy, and money you spend on it), it is an idol.

Before Amberle went blind at age twenty-one, she believed she had been called into missions. She was fully devoted to that calling—doing summer mission work, studying to be a nurse, teaching Sunday school, and volunteering with underserved populations. It wasn't until she became blind, however, when God seemingly removed her ability to be a missionary, that she realized that her desire to serve God had become an idol. Amberle had been more focused on *serving* God than on *God* himself.

An idol may be a job, money, a relationship, a degree of success, a solution to a problem, or a dream. In my case, I wanted my daughter to be healed; in Amberle's case, she wanted to be a missionary. While nothing was wrong with either of those desires—and more than likely, nothing is wrong with the desires you currently hold, desires must have their proper place—*after* God.

Idolatry is not always blatant. It doesn't necessarily mean you stop worshipping God. It may simply mean you have a divided heart (Matthew 6:24). Even so, God is extremely clear about the fact that He is a jealous God (Exodus 20:5), and He wants and deserves your whole heart (Deuteronomy 6:5).

Having an idol of the heart means that you feel as if you need something *in addition* to God to feel satisfied. Therefore, you look elsewhere. You ponder the problem, fixate on the fear, or desire the dream. Ultimately, you spend more time and more energy thinking about the situation than the Savior. In other words, you unintentionally reverse your priorities and become willing to settle for a solution rather than God's sovereignty.

It takes a great deal of humility to realize that you

have created an idol in your heart, but once you've recognized the misappropriation of your energies, through God's mercy and grace, you can reorder it.

One more thing: I am not saying you should ignore something that is important to you. God invites us to bring our supplications before Him because He *can* take care of it, and by bringing our requests before Him, we prioritize faith over fear. Philippians 4:6 reminds us, "Do not be anxious about anything, but in every situation, by prayer and petition, with thanksgiving, present your requests to God."

So, pray about whatever is on your heart, but place it before God and concentrate on hearing Him. It's not about realizing a solution; it's about recognizing God's sovereignty—His goodness, His faithfulness, and His love.

The Waiting Room

...but those who wait for the LORD shall renew their strength; they shall mount up with wings like eagles; they shall run and not be weary; they shall walk and not faint.
(Isaiah 40:31 ESV)

Waiting. For something to change. For an answer to prayer. For the problem to pass. Regardless of your current situation, I bet you're waiting for something. After all, the average person spends five years just waiting in line and there's a lot more to waiting than just paying for groceries or purchasing a movie ticket.

Waiting is exhausting. Whether you're waiting for something joyous such as a birth or a marriage, or something that brings a heavier concern like the results of a medical test or a job offer, waiting zaps our energy.

Waiting increases anxiety because waiting implies change and change is unknown. Whenever we don't know something, we become stressed and stress drains us emotionally and physically. Waiting can also be frustrating because, as selfish human beings, we want everything our way! We live in a results-oriented, my-way-or-the-highway, immediate-gratification society, and we want results now . . . if not sooner!

But life doesn't work that way.

Scripture teaches the right way to wait . . . and it's not about anticipating an event. As today's verse teaches, it's about waiting on the Lord. When you wait for an event, you become weary because you want to be in control. Since that will never happen, expecting an event (although it will eventually occur) is an unproductive effort.

Waiting on the Lord is a different matter. When you wait for the Lord, you surrender to His sovereignty. You accept His timing and His plans (even though you may not be happy about it), and you look to Christ instead of the consequence. When you trust the Lord instead of your circumstances, the stress seems to disappear. In fact, Scripture indicates that the reward of waiting on the Lord isn't just that your anxiety dissipates; waiting on the Lord actually improves your physical, mental, and spiritual state.

So what does "waiting on the Lord" look like "in the flesh?" Well, it's about more than patience; it's about priority. Waiting on the Lord looks like someone whose need for God is greater than his need for results. Waiting on the Lord looks like someone who knows the value of endurance—someone who understands that "when you have done the will of God, you will receive what he has promised" (Hebrews 10:36).

Since waiting on the Lord does not come naturally, God gives us plenty of opportunities to develop it. Sometimes *when* something happens is actually more important than *what* happens because we're learning how to wait. The more you trust God during the tranquil times, however, the easier it will be to wait on Him during the tough ones.

So, when you're in the waiting room of life, be purposeful. Allow God to teach you to wait on Him. You don't have to become anxious about the unknown or confused by your questions. Take those thoughts captive (2 Corinthians 10:5) and set your mind on things above (Colossians 3:2). Instead of becoming frustrated about the future, break free of it. God is waiting for us to learn to wait on Him.

Uncovering "Ouchies"

*Search me, God, and know my heart; test me and
know my anxious thoughts. See if there is any offensive
way in me, and lead me in the way everlasting.*
(Psalm 139:23-24)

I heard the clatter of the bicycle falling to the ground,
followed immediately by a high-pitched scream.

"Mom! Help!"

I skidded to a stop and looked behind me. Twenty
feet away was my was my five-year-old daughter in her
Bugs Bunny bike helmet, with tears streaming down
her cheeks, grasping what I could tell was another
skinned knee.

"What happened?" I pedaled back toward her.

"I fell," Christina said through sobs.

That was obvious. What was not so evident, however,
was the extent of her injury. I quickly dismounted. "Oh
honey," I said sympathetically. "I'm sorry. Let me see
your boo-boo."

"Noooooo," she wailed, reacting as if I'd just asked
if I could amputate her leg.

"Honey, it's a boo-boo." I used my most comforting
tone. "Mama needs to see it so she can help you."

"No! It's going to hurt," she protested as she curled up like a roly-poly.

"Please? I'll be gentle." I couldn't lie to her. Yes, an antibiotic spray would sting for a moment, and if she had a deep cut, she might need stitches.

Finally, after ten minutes of my cajoling, Christina slowly uncurled and removed her hand from her knee so that I could assess the damage.

We're that way with God, too. We have a "boo-boo" or an "ouchie"—at least, that's what we call it, but it's really a sin—a choice we've made that separates us from God. He asks us to admit it—to show it to Him. But we want to keep it covered.

We tell God, "No, please don't look at it. If I show it to You, You won't love me anymore or You'll punish me and that's really going to hurt!"

Whether it's a sore or a sin, things have to be exposed to be healed.

We need to approach God like David did in today's verses, asking Him daily to expose our sins.

For all of us—Christians or non-Christians—shame and pride keep us from admitting our sin. Yet God knows about it already, and He still loves us.

Shame is the surface emotion of fear. Deep down, we're afraid that God will reject us if we sin, but that's a lie from the enemy. And pride is the oldest sin in the book. Pride says, "I don't need God. I'm responsible for myself. I don't need to admit any wrong."

Are you imprisoned by pride or living in the shadow of shame, refusing to take responsibility for your sin? God exposes our sin because He loves us. He'd rather do so privately, but if you insist, he'll do it publicly, because God will do whatever it takes to bring you to Him and give you the freedom that He paid for when He died on the cross.

God shows you your sins so you can kiss them goodbye—well, maybe not kiss them but certainly get rid of them and kick them to the curb. 1 John 1:9 promises: "If we confess our sins, he is faithful and just and will forgive us our sins and purify us from all unrighteousness."

Taking responsibility for our boo-boos is hard, but it's critical for a healthy Christian walk. God knows our secret sins, yet He still loves us. We need to remove our hands from our ouchies and bring our sins before Him so He can remove them. God won't take them away until we give them to Him, but once we do, he "removes them" (Psalm 103:12), "forgets them" (Hebrews 8:12), and "covers them" (Romans 4:7-8). Yes, it may be painful—sins have consequences—but it is always better to break free from the bondage of our sins, and let the healing begin.

A Miracle for Me

"And I will do whatever you ask in my name, so that the Father may be glorified in the Son. You may ask me for anything in my name, and I will do it."
(John 14:13-14)

If you're going through a trial right now, chances are that the title of this devotion has a rather paradoxical effect on you. While you'd love to hear about a miracle, what you really want isn't a miracle for me, but a miracle for *you*!

Right now, I have an intercessory prayer list with at least twenty needs on it. I'm praying for each one of those needs. Experience tells me that some of those situations will resolve in exactly the way I am requesting; others will not.

In today's verses, Jesus promises that we can ask for anything in His name and He will do it. Later, in 1 John, that pledge is restated: "If we ask anything according to His will, he hears us. And we know that he hears us—whatever we ask—we know that we have what we asked of him" (1 John 5:14-15).

Every believer wants to believe that promise. We know it's the truth. It's Scripture. But we may not see it. And that's the problem: the way we see . . . or perhaps more accurately, the way we *don't* see. We have to stop having such a small vision of miracles!

Five years ago, my daughter went blind. Every day since then, my husband and I have asked God to help her in tangible ways. We've also asked Him to heal her. Every single day. A couple of weeks ago, as I was praying, I received this word. I believe it was from the Holy Spirit: "There are other things more important than healing."

It was a hard word, but it was true.

There are many things that are more important than physical healing: joy, peace, contentment, love—to name a few. I know many physically healthy individuals who are severely handicapped by a critical spirit, toxic anger, and constant dissatisfaction. Yet my daughter, a blind nurse who is serving in medical missions, is miraculously joyful, miraculously capable, and miraculously content.

I praised God for the miracle.

God *always* answers our prayers for a miracle. That's what Scripture promises. So how do you reconcile that truth with what you *don't* see is what you *do* get?

Many times, when we pray for miracles, we pray for external needs: things we can see, touch, or feel— because we live in a world of physical and material needs.

Sometimes, however, God doesn't answer our prayer externally; He answers it internally. God hears our request and determines the best possible overall outcome—not just for you and me, but for everyone. Yes, Father really does know best. That may mean that God doesn't always give us the miracle we want, but He will always give us the miracle we need.

When we only pray for miracles that we want, expecting only certain results, we actually limit God. Expectations can become limitations. We put miracles in a box instead of recognizing that God and His ways cannot be contained by the human mind. Perhaps instead of an external healing, the true miracle is the way He draws us closer to Him or the way He increases our faith. Perhaps instead of an external "win" in the job market, the true miracle is in learning to trust Him in the little things, or in receiving strength and grace to live another day.

As God works those incredible, customized miracles for each of His children, we also receive the extraordinary blessing that God knows each of us by name. While I do love a good "external miracle" in which God shows Himself to the world, I think that ultimately, I enjoy an "internal miracle" even more because I don't just get to see God's intervention; I get to experience it!

When a believer asks for a miracle, there's no way he can lose because God *always* answers the prayer of His child. Oh, that we would have the faith to believe that God can do what He says He can do and that we would see God at work as we open the eyes of our heart (Ephesians 1:18)!

God's way is always best, and if God does not grant our specific request, we know He will perform an even greater miracle! Friend, we cannot lose when we seek God in prayer because just the process of coming before Him and seeking Him increases our intimacy with Him. That is a miracle in itself—a miracle for me *and* you.

The Perfect Paradox

*But the fruit of the Spirit is love, joy, peace,
forbearance, kindness, goodness, faithfulness,
gentleness and self-control. Against such
things there is no law.*
(Galatians 5:22-23)

L ife is a paradox. Whether we're dealing with
physical, mental, or spiritual challenges, difficult
experiences seem to give birth to the greatest growth.

Galatians 5:22-23 lists the quintessential
characteristics of every Christian—nine "must haves"
for all who claim Jesus as Lord—also known as the
fruit of the Spirit: love, joy, peace, patience, kindness,
goodness, faithfulness, gentleness, and self-control.
The wording "fruit of the Spirit" is quite intentional
here because, although the Holy Spirit gives us the
seeds of this nine-fold fruit when He comes to live
inside us, the fruit grows and develops during seasons
of a Christian's life.

During the harshest season of the year, a tree or
vine appears to be dormant and there is no visible fruit.
Unseen, however, below the surface of the ground,
the plant is actually gaining strength in its root system

for the coming spring. When the time arrives and the conditions are right, the plant will bud and bear much fruit.

In John 15:5, as Jesus spoke to His disciples, He compared himself to a fruit-bearing vine: "I am the vine; you are the branches. If you remain in me and I in you, you will bear much fruit; apart from me you can do nothing."

Think about it. We don't cultivate permanent peace when everything is going our way. Peace ripens when our personal world is at war, and we feel attacked on all sides.

Lasting patience is never propagated when we have plenty of time. We develop patience when we're in a rush, running late, and trying not to explode.

Love does not enlarge when we associate with caring, kindhearted friends. Love matures when we cope with Sister Cranky, Brother Grumpy, and Mr. Grouchy.

In the midst of the worst possible circumstances, the seeds of the fruit of the Holy Spirit are nurtured so that, when we need to, we can bear the type of fruit that Christ commands: "fruit that will last" (John 15:16).

Several years ago, I was having some real difficulty with a so-called friend. She wasn't being very nice and honestly, neither was I. I felt as if I'd done nothing to deserve her antagonism. After one particularly stinging event, I remember sitting in the car, pouring out my heart to God, asking, "Why does this always happen to me?"

Out of nowhere, I sensed God speaking. "Fertilizer."

I drew a deep breath. "What?"

"Fertilizer," came the answer.

If you know anything about the makeup of fertilizer (hint: animal dung—and that's exactly what I thought about this situation at the time), you'll appreciate God's humor in my time of "distress." As I sensed God trying to relieve my earthbound agony by putting things into His heavenly perspective with a wit that only my Abba Daddy could pull off, I laughed and realized that God really did have a purpose for this momentary hardship. I would grow from the experience. Looking back, that event nurtured my abilities to love, forgive, and endure. And just for the record, my friend and I are now closer than ever.

The paradox of life is that challenging times bring the greatest growth. Human suffering, big or small, is a tool that God always uses for His purpose. He never lets it go unused. The book of Hebrews tells us that this was true even for Jesus: "Even though Jesus was God's Son, he learned obedience from the things He suffered" (Hebrews 5:8 NLT).

When life is hard and you feel like you're waist deep in fertilizer, ask yourself, "How is God growing me right now?" Let the Gardener of your soul till the soil in your heart so that He can bring forth a harvest in your spirit.

Why Don't You
Do Something?

*For our light and momentary troubles are achieving
for us an eternal glory that far outweighs them all.*
(2 Corinthians 4:17)

Christians know that God can do anything. And God knows it, too. In Jeremiah 32:27, the Lord proclaims, "I am the LORD, the God of all mankind. Is anything too hard for me?"

The answer to that question, of course, is unequivocally, "No, nothing is too difficult for you, Lord." Perhaps that's why, in the midst of my frustration and failure, I've sometimes asked God, "If nothing is too difficult for you, Lord, then why don't you *do* something? Why don't you take away the pain, remove the suffering, and make it all better?" Yes, I've thought that, and I bet you have, too.

As Christians, when we're having a difficult time, we turn to God—as we certainly should, although sometimes, He's our last resort! We beg Jesus for a supernatural solution—a resolution to our rough patch—because we know He can fix it!

And sometimes, God does. God miraculously

intervenes, and the problem disappears. More often, however, He doesn't—or perhaps more accurately, God doesn't *appear* to intervene. In reality, God is *always* in the midst of our trials, working on our behalf. However, because He is working in the way we *need*—not necessarily in the way we *want*—we may not always be aware of His involvement.

Our tendency is to think, *If you loved me, Lord, you would do this for me.* In other words, we determine God's love based on a temporary situation rather than an eternal truth. God's Word promises that God *is* "abounding in love and faithfulness" (Psalm 86:15) and, in fact, that "God *is* love" (1 John 4:8). As a child of God, you can be assured that God loves you—all the time—although, when you are in a difficult circumstance, it may not look like it, and it certainly won't feel like it.

Sometimes God permits pain to bring us closer to Him or allows tests to show us inconsistencies in our faith. God may grant trials to teach us about His faithfulness. Whatever the case, God cares more about our connection with Him than our comfort. And while God does not *cause* pain and suffering (it's actually either the consequence of our sin or an attack from the enemy), He may allow misery in our lives in order to strengthen our relationship with Him.

But we don't see that. We only see the agony of the here and now—what Paul referred to as our "light and momentary troubles" (2 Corinthians 4:17). And yet, Paul assures us that these troubles are not what they seem; in fact, they are beneficial because they are "achieving for us an eternal glory that far outweighs them all" (2 Corinthians 4:17).

As Christians, we need to be less focused on the outcome of our situation and more focused on our obedience. It's not *God* who needs to do something; it's *us*. Do we need to trust God more? Love others like we love ourselves? Take responsibility and ask forgiveness for an ongoing sin?

On the cross, Jesus proclaimed, "It is finished" (John 19:30). And yet, unsolved problems, unsaved people, and untold pain still existed—and they still do today. So how can "it" possibly be "finished?" What did Jesus mean?

Simply, Jesus meant that *His* work was done. He had completed the job that the Father sent Him to do. When Jesus died on the cross for our sins, God gave mankind the unsurpassed gift of forgiveness as well as the opportunity to live an abundant life both in heaven and on earth. He made a way for you and me to become children of God. And that is more than enough—at least, it should be. Even if God never "does" another thing for you, it has to be okay. Because Christ has already done it all. It *is* finished!

What Can I Say?

*Carry each other's burdens, and in this
way you will fulfill the law of Christ.*
(Galatians 6:2)

Life can be awkward—especially when a friend is experiencing difficult circumstances . . . and I can only relate on a cognitive level. When a friend loses a child, gets a divorce, or is overwhelmed by an experience that I have never endured, sometimes I feel like I only open my mouth to change feet. My heart is crying, but my words are insufficient. How can I sincerely support my friend without appearing superficial?

When my family faced its most significant challenge, many well-meaning, Christian friends tried to comfort us. They'd say things like, "Oh, it's only a little bump in the road" or "This is just a small interruption. Things will be back to normal in no time." But they were wrong. And the sting of their comforting-but-unintentionally- dismissive words threatened to burden me with bitterness.

God gave us the body of Christ to love one another in difficult times—to be the hands and feet of Jesus.

Sometimes, we are able to use a former trial that we have experienced in order to comfort someone else (2 Corinthians 1:3-5). Other times, however, the best thing a friend can do is just be there. A friend can't take away the pain, but a friend can say, "I love you" simply by being present.

I sat in the hospital room for hours while my daughter drifted in and out of consciousness. Every day, friends came. Just to be there. They didn't try to "cheer us up" or "get our mind off the situation." They carried our burdens by mourning with us. Sometimes we cried, and sometimes we prayed. Sometimes they listened to me as I reminisced about the good times, but usually, they were silent. Still, with their presence, they demonstrated that our family was greatly loved.

When Job was suffering, his three friends visited him, intending to comfort him (Job 2:11). When they saw the extent of Job's tragedy, however, all they could do was mourn with him. And that was enough (Job 2:12-13).

In fact, when Job's friends finally did try to comfort Job by using their words, they made things worse. Their feeble attempts to explain the cause of Job's pain actually demonstrated their superficial understanding of the situation. They assumed that Job was to blame for his tragic situation and insisted that he repent of a sin he had never committed. God ultimately condemned the three friends for their erroneous opinions (Job 42:7).

We can learn a lot from Job's friends about not making faulty assumptions or false accusations. But we can also learn about the importance of just being there for a hurting friend.

As a member of the body of Christ, we may not always know what to say or do to help one another. However, it is better to risk doing it wrong than to do nothing at all. Bringing love to a friend who is desperate for God is reflective of the gospel because "love never fails" (1 Corinthians 13:8).

Philippians 4:13 says, "I can do all things through him who gives me strength." Yet, much less familiar, in the very next verse, Paul writes, "Yet it was good of you to share in my troubles." We *can* do all things through Christ who gives us strength, but it is a blessing to have a brother or sister in Christ hold our hand as we walk through it.

About the Author

Glenda Durano loves to share life lessons through speaking, writing, teaching, and mentoring. An award-winning speaker and television director, multiple business owner, lifelong educator, author, and church staff member, Glenda considers her most significant accomplishments to be the roles she quietly attempts to fulfill each day—being a godly wife, mother, and friend.

After homeschooling for twenty years, in 2009, Glenda combined her diverse professional background in marketing, management, and communication with her love of education and created College Advising and Planning Services, a full-service, faith-based educational consulting firm that helps students navigate the college planning process. Glenda also serves as the Children's Choir Director at Calvary Chapel, Albuquerque, where she directs the annual children's Christmas "praise-entation," which utilizes over 100 kindergarten through fifth grade children. Glenda heads up the prayer ministry for a weekly community Bible Study and enjoys traveling and speaking. Glenda has been married to D. C. Durano for 31 years. They have two amazing daughters, Christina and Amberle, who are both married to equally amazing young men.

With this book, Glenda desires to demonstrate God's faithfulness, goodness, and sovereignty and encourage readers that they are not alone in their trials. God *always* acts out of love for His children—although sometimes it's hard to see it in the midst of a trial or tragedy.

If you'd like to read more about Glenda's daughter's experience with Toxic Epidermal Necrolysis, go to www.amberlesjourney.weebly.com, or if you have a question or comment regarding something in this book, please send her an email at glendadurano@gmail.com.

May we all remain "desperate for God."